YOUR
HIDDEN
FREEDOM

THE ULTIMATE FORCE

JOHN OLIVER BRUNELLE

BALBOA.PRESS

A DIVISION OF HAY HOUSE

Balboa Press books may be ordered through booksellers or by contacting:

Balboa Press
A Division of Hay House
1663 Liberty Drive
Bloomington, IN 47403
www.balboapress.com
1 (877) 407-4847

Print information available on the last page.

ISBN: 978-1-9822-4192-6 (sc)
ISBN: 978-1-9822-4194-0 (hc)
ISBN: 978-1-9822-4193-3 (e)

Library of Congress Control Number: 2020901488

Balboa Press rev. date: 01/24/2020

CONTENTS

THE SITUATION YOU ARE IN

You have an underlying desire that demands satisfaction, but you do not know what it is that you desire.

As a child you were curious about everything in your search for what would satisfy that desire.

Then your body matured and you experienced sexual desire and satisfaction which is always irresistibly addictive and can convince you, for a period of time that it is the satisfaction that you are searching for, but sexual satisfaction is always only a momentary satisfaction and sexual desire and ability wanes as your body ages. You eventually realize that sexual satisfaction is not the satisfaction that you seek.

Your family and friends usually give you the greatest satisfaction that you ever experience, but friends in the mobile, fluid world that you are subject to, often disappear or lose their relevance in your life and the intimate satisfaction of the family ends when that intimacy disintegrates from the force of change that time always demands.

What the world can provide in comfort, pleasure and protection shows great promise of being able to satisfy you, and seems to provide others the satisfaction you seek. So you passionately pursue satisfaction from what the world can provide, but no matter how much pleasure, comfort, protection and security that you are able to experience, it never succeeds in satisfying you.

Wealth, power, comfort, pleasure, sex, protection, security, fame, family, friends, occupation, accomplishments, knowledge, philosophy and religion are never able to satisfy you. To avoid experiencing your continuing dissatisfaction, you keep yourself busy with your work and your personal activities.

You eventually realize that you are not going to achieve the satisfaction you seek, and you may resign yourself to this fact. Not being satisfied is not the best situation, but it is better than suffering, but suffering cannot be avoided in the world you must contend with.

As your body begins to succumb to age, disease and injury, you soon realize that no matter what you do, you are unable to keep yourself from suffering. It is not just the problems, discomfort and pain of an aging body that you experience. You begin to experience your underlying dissatisfaction more intensely as your body loses its ability to pursue your work and routines of diversion.

Even when you finally realize that your plan of using what the world in which you struggle can provide to achieve satisfaction and stop your suffering, is not going to succeed, you still believe that it is, although inadequate, the best you can do in the situation that you are in, and you simply endure your continuing and increasing dissatisfaction and suffering.

The more you focus on the situation that you are in, the more you will realize that if there is a solution to your dissatisfaction and suffering, it is not contained within the cause and effect logic of the world in which you struggle. You need a force that overrules the cause and effect logic of the world in which you struggle; a force that would give you the freedom to create and attract the events you desire to experience.

You and every human are already in possession of such a force. You may have noticed that some people seem to always be lucky and some people seem to always be unlucky, and everyone else seems to be on a treadmill continually experiencing the same tone of positive and negative events during their entire life.

Why do the events each human experiences have such incredible consistency? Shouldn't the luck of the draw (the probabilities of your world) create many more varied positive and negative events in an individual's life?

The reason it does not is that you and every other human being are, without being aware of it, creating and attracting all of the events of their life and the circumstances that make those events either positive or negative.

You need the enlightenment of a pure understanding of the situation you are in, why you are in that situation and how you can extricate yourself from the situation that you are in. You need to discover the hidden attributes and logic of your true nature.

ENLIGHTENMENT –
PURE UNDERSTANDING

Your present absolute belief in the cause and effect logic of the world in which you struggle is your biggest obstacle to discovering how you attract and control the events and circumstances of your life and control the effect of what you create.

Your intelligence is captive of that logic because that logic seems to have been continually validated by all of the events of your life and everybody else's life, but it is only your intelligence that can discover how you attract and control all of the events and circumstances of your life.

Your intelligence must discover a different logic, with different premises, that directs a force that supersedes the cause and effect logic of the world in which you struggle.

Because that logic so completely contradicts the logic of the limited and negative world in which you struggle, it is extremely difficult for your intelligence, that has been captive of the cause and effect logic of that world for your entire life, to even consider its existence, but only your intelligence can lead you in this quest.

The intelligence of most people is so captive of the logic of the world in which you struggle, that it is almost impossible for them to even consider the possibility that a force that encompasses and contradicts the logic of that world exists, but there is considerable evidence, some of it indisputable, of the effect of a human's expectations on their bodies and on the elements of Nature that cannot be explained by the cause and effect logic of the world in which you struggle. There is enough evidence for your intelligence to discover the truth of your nature.

You will discover that the hidden power of every human being to attract and affect events has a degree of probability that will cause your intelligence to seriously consider and explore its possible existence.

For your intelligence to discover the ability of your expectations to attract and affect events will require a willingness for you to set aside the logic that seems to have been validated by all of the events of your life to pursue the possibility of a different logic.

You do not need to be an intellectual to discover your true nature, understand the situation that you are really in, and how you can change that situation, for the truth is not complex. It is very simple. It is not difficult to understand, but it is difficult to discover, for it is hidden and for a very good reason which you will discover. It is not possible to understand your nature, the attributes of your nature and the situation that you are in by using the cause and effect logic of the world in which you struggle.

An Indian Shaman, who was a Shaman's Shaman, whose knowledge and understanding of many things impressed me many years ago, once stated, in no uncertain terms, that true enlightenment is always the product of impeccable reasoning, which seemed to me, at the time, to be a very unlikely thing for an Indian Shaman steeped in Indian lore to say, but he did not call it enlightenment. For him enlightenment was pure understanding. Faith or trust that relies on the ability of someone else to tell you what the truth is cannot produce pure understanding. Your intelligence is the only source of pure understanding. With this in mind, let us begin your journey of enlightenment that will lead you to a pure understanding of the situation that you are in, why you are in that situation and what you need to do to improve the situation you are in. There will be no unanswered questions.

You are searching for the ability to create and attract events that will satisfy you and prevent you from suffering.

You may be aware that there is a mountain of evidence that your expectations as to the health of your body can have a dramatic effect on the health of your body, but you are not likely to be aware that there is also considerable evidence that your expectations can have a direct effect on the elements in the world of Nature.

THE PLACEBO EFFECT
THE ABILITY OF HUMAN
EXPECTATIONS TO AFFECT THE
HEALTH OF THEIR BODIES

There is massive evidence that the expectations of an ordinary person can cause their body to heal itself that has been factually verified thousands and thousands of times.

A new drug, to validate its effectiveness, is always scientifically tested by giving the drug to a controlled group of people that have a physical problem that the drug is expected to control, diminish or eliminate, or is expected to prevent them from developing, but only one-half of the group is given the drug. The other one-half is given a harmless ineffective sugar pill that is called a placebo.

It is necessary to test drugs in this way because it has been discovered from thousands of tests of drugs, that if a person taking a drug has an intense level of expectation that the drug will cure or benefit them, then it will cure or benefit them, even though the drug being tested later proves to be absolutely ineffective.

None of the members of the group testing the effectiveness of a drug know whether they are taking the drug or a placebo and most do not know that they may be taking a placebo rather than the drug that is being tested.

To prevent the interpretation of the results of the test from being in any way affected by the expectations and desires of those who are conducting the test, the individuals conducting the test usually do not know who is taking the drug and who is taking the placebo.

Some members of the test group that are taking the placebo always experience benefits from taking the placebo. These benefits are far greater than is statistically possible from unknown factors and this occurs over and over. Because of this, those who are taking the drug rather than the placebo must, as a group, benefit significantly more from the drug than those taking the placebo, for the drug to be considered effective.

Because of the placebo effect, every new drug would initially appear to be somewhat effective if this testing procedure was not used. The placebo effect is irrefutable scientific evidence that your expectations have a direct effect on the energy, fiber, healing and health of your physical body, but this has to be a special expectation, for almost everyone testing a drug expects to benefit from the drug, but only some of those taking the placebo do benefit from the placebo.

Because it is created by an expectation of benefit, the placebo effect can also be created by any kind of physical manipulation of the body, incantation or spell that causes the recipient to experience an expectation of benefit. Because of the placebo effect, people can and do benefit from strange, bizarre and unscientific cures.

The personality, demeanor and magnetism of some individuals are so strong, dominant and persuasive that they can greatly influence the expectations of others and cause their expectations to affect the health of their bodies. Healers of many persuasions have been credited with healing many afflictions. Because of the placebo effect, a medical doctor, in whom you have great confidence, is more likely to cure you than one in which you have little or no confidence.

There is little dispute that an optimistic attitude promotes good health and the recovery of health from illness or injury, and a pessimistic attitude promotes illness, the continuation of illness and the inability or difficulty of recovering from illness or injury.

The nocebo effect is the exact opposite of the placebo effect. The nocebo effect is the actual detrimental effect on the health of an individual's body, from that person simply believing that a substance, action or situation has injured them, even though scientific testing conclusively determines that the substance, action or situation could not have injured them.

If the placebo effect exists, and there is no doubt that it does, it is only reasonable to believe that the nocebo effect also exists. The nocebo effect has been observed many times. It has been the source of considerable litigation by those claiming to be injured by a substance, action or situation that could not have injured them.

That humans have attributes that they are not aware of is supported by the recent discovery that if a human imagines over and over that they are doing the scales on a piano, that their skill performing the scales will be enhanced and their brain will physically change to reflect this enhanced skill.

There is no question that your expectations can have a dramatic effect on the health and well-being of your body both positively and negatively. Is there any evidence that your expectations can affect the elements that comprise the world of Nature?

THE ABILITY OF HUMAN EXPECTATIONS TO AFFECT THE ELEMENTS IN THE WORLD OF NATURE

Quantum Physics has discovered by observation that the electrons that comprise the atom, that are the source of all energy in the world of Nature, will directly respond to human expectations. This just about covers everything in the world of Nature, but there is even more evidence of the elements of Nature responding to human expectations.

Scientists have discovered in their study of sunlight, that if sunlight is measured as a particle of matter, it becomes a particle of matter, but if it is measured as a wave of energy, it becomes a wave of energy. This is considered to be scientifically impossible, but sunlight always responds in this way to the expectation of the human measuring it.

Creative visualization is an activity that appears to give some people the ability to control the movement of an object such as a baseball when they throw it at a target.

Before the ball is thrown, the person throwing the ball mentally visualizes the flight of the ball and where it will hit the target. This significantly improves the ability of some people to control the flight of a ball just as the placebo effect causes some people to heal their body. Not all expectations are equal. The placebo here is the mental visualization of the flight of the ball before it is thrown.

There is also evidence that human expectations can affect the purity of water.

It was discovered by Dr. Masaru Emoto of Japan that the greater the purity of water, the more beautiful the pattern of the ice crystals formed by the water will be when it is frozen. Snowflakes, in their consummate natural purity, always have incredibly beautiful patterns. Contaminated water always creates ugly patterned crystals when it is frozen.

Dr. Emoto began his experiments believing that harmonic thoughts would purify contaminated water. To prove this, he directed harmonious words, symbols and music at contaminated water for a period of time and when the water was then frozen, it formed beautiful crystals. The water had been purified. Something had purified the water. His findings were well documented in several books that Dr. Emoto wrote regarding his experiments to purify contaminated water. Dr. Emoto eventually concluded that it was his personal expectations, not harmonic thoughts that had purified the water, just as a human expectation created by a placebo can cause a human to heal their body.

Dr. Emoto discovered the ability of human expectations to directly affect the most dominant substance in the world of Nature – Water. Others have claimed to have duplicated his findings.

The scientific method of duplicating a discovery to confirm its validity is not available to validate the power of human expectations, for the quality and intensity of a human expectation cannot be quantified or measured. A human expectation cannot be put in a test tube.

The power of human expectations is not without its advocates. It is generally accepted that a person who is confident of succeeding in some endeavor whether it is a physical or a non-physical endeavor, is more likely to succeed than a person who is fearful of failing. Confident expectations are generally considered to be more likely to create positive events and fearful expectations are generally considered to be more likely to create negative events.

It cannot be scientifically validated whether an individual's confidence or fear can directly affect the events they experience or if their confidence or fear simply causes them to perform better or worse and causes others to respond differently to their actions, for there is no way of measuring the intensity or quality of an individual's confidence or fear.

That we are attracting or affecting with our expectations (thoughts) far more of the events that we experience than we realize is not new. Many highly esteemed beings have said or implied this. The Buddha said *"All that we are is a result of what we have thought."* Seth, the being that spoke through Jane Roberts said *"You create your own reality."* Hazrat Inayat Khan, the Sufi Master, said *"Every man is the creator of his own conditions, favorable or unfavorable."* Don Juan Matus, the Yaqui Indian Shaman who was Carlos Castaneda's teacher, said that each of us lives in a bubble and the walls of that bubble always reflect back to us our view of the world no matter what that view is for it is how we view the world that creates our world. The famous clairvoyant Edgar Casey said substantially the same thing when he said *"All you ever do in this life is meet yourself."* The Course in Miracles makes it very clear that you are directly responsible for all the events that you experience. Christ made it very clear on several occasions that it was the faith of the one who had benefited from a miracle that Christ had apparently performed, that had actually caused the miracle to occur. Faith is an expectation.

Some spiritual leaders, when pressed to define evil, declare to the consternation of their followers that evil does not exist. This could only be true if each of us is somehow always creating or attracting whatever we experience. Evil requires an unwilling victim. If we are somehow creating our own suffering, we unknowingly become willing victims and evil does not exist.

Those who are regarded to have the deepest understanding of the Karmic law of Eastern tradition believe that you will experience, in the events of your life, the quality of the energy that you are expressing in your thoughts, expectations and actions. This makes your thoughts, expectations and actions responsible for the events you experience.

The Bible says *"You reap what you sow."* This very much resembles the Karmic belief that you are creating the events that you are experiencing with your thoughts, expectations and actions.

If you have the ability to create, attract and affect events with your expectations, where did you get that ability?

WHERE HUMANS GOT THE ABILITY TO CREATE, ATTRACT AMD AFFECT EVENTS WITH THEIR EXPECTATIONS

Science has concluded that evolution is the source of all human attributes and that evolution is the result of the random mutations of the physical attributes of a species of life when it reproduces itself. Science has also concluded that a human expectation is the product of the brain using probabilities and previous events to predict a future event and that the only power that a human expectation has is that it can cause you to act or not to act, but acknowledges that it can somehow, sometimes cause the body to heal itself (the placebo effect). These are rational conclusions using the cause and effect logic of the world of Nature as the source of all human attributes, but totally disregards the evidence that human expectations can have a direct effect on the elements that comprise the world of Nature. You need to totally understand the theory of evolution to continue your journey to a pure understanding of the situation you are in.

When a species of life reproduces itself, it usually replicates itself, which preserves its existing physical ability to survive, but a species of life does not always replicate itself.

Sometimes the offspring of a species of life will have a physical attribute that that species of life did not previously have or will not have a physical attribute that that species of life previously had. These are believed to be random, chance mutations of a species' physical attributes and thus cannot be predicted. These random mutations are believed to be the source of all of the physical attributes of the life in the world of Nature.

The results of these random mutations are then either magnified and preserved or eliminated by what Darwin describes as the Law of Natural Selection.

The Law of Natural Selection is based on the simple fact that an offspring of a species of life that has a beneficial mutation of its physical attributes that enable it to better survive, will be more likely to survive and replicate itself and its new beneficial physical attribute in its offspring than an offspring of that species of life without that beneficial physical attribute. This is the law of the jungle, which is simply "The survival of the fittest."

The constant evolution of all of the species of life in the world of Nature is thus constantly improving their ability to survive.

Evolution and the Law of Natural Selection eliminates the need for there to be any intelligent design for all of the physical attributes of all of the species of life in the world of Nature to exist, but is an expectation of a human that directly affects the health of their body and the elements in the world of Nature a physical attribute? There is nothing tangible about an expectation. It cannot be measured or quantified. Could physical evolution produce what cannot be measured or quantified? There is no evidence that the expectations of other animals or other species of life can affect the health of their bodies or the elements in Nature.

If human expectation can do this, physical evolution does not seem to be a likely source of such an attribute. A non-physical, intelligent, creative Being would be a far more likely source of such an attribute.

Is there any evidence that such a Being exists? The existence of design in the world of Nature would be evidence of such a Being. The incredibly intricately beneficial attributes of the species of life in the world of Nature that features the monumental human brain that can rewire itself to restore mobility to an injured limb, certainly have the appearance of being designed. Many people believe there is design in the world of Nature, but it is impossible to limit in any way the physical attributes that billions and billions of mutations of millions and millions of species of life over billions and billions of years could create. The random physical evolution of the species of life in the world of Nature could have produced every physical attribute of the species of life in the world of Nature. The apparent existence of design in the physical attributes of the species of life in the world of Nature is not proof that they were designed. The theory of evolution producing all of the physical attributes of the species of life in the world of Nature will always be a very, very strong possibility.

But design does not always cause something to happen. Design can also prevent something from happening. One of the effects of evolution contradicts the ability of evolution to eventually create any physical attribute, and instead has caused the attributes of the many species of life in the world of Nature to be very harmonic regarding the survival of other species of life, which has created a mammoth diversity of species of life in the world of Nature.

If Evolution and Natural Selection can produce the incredibly intricate attributes of the millions of species of life in the world of Nature that enables virtually all of them to survive in a very competitive and dangerous world, it should have also produced a number of predatory species of life that are so dominant and prolific that they would eliminate most other species of life in the world of Nature. Where are the super predators?

Super predators would be far more likely for evolution to produce than the incredibly intricately beneficial human brain, as well as many other intricately beneficial attributes of the life in the world of Nature, for a super predator does not need much intelligence or exceptionally complex attributes.

All a super predator needs is some combination of size, strength, speed, weapons (claws, teeth, and venom), the ability to digest most life and a way of locating its prey (sight, smell, and hearing). A short period of gestation, early maturity, a long life span and multiple offspring could easily create a super predator from a talented predator, but such predators do not exist.

Evolution can create the incredibly complex human brain, but does not create super predators?

Many people and cultures have recognized that there seems to be an underlying harmony in the competitive conflict of the species of life in the world of Nature that enables virtually every species of life to successfully survive and express their diverse and sometimes conflicting natures.

This very vexing contradiction of evolution's ability to create every imaginable physical attribute, but does not produce super predators, presents the distinct possibility of intelligent design in the species of life in the world of Nature and thus the possibility that a Being of some magnitude created that world and a very strong probability that the ability of human expectations to directly affect the health of their bodies and the elements in the world of Nature could be an attribute that humans got from such a Being. Impeccable reasoning demands that that possibility be fully explored.

DISCOVERING THE NATURE AND ATTRIBUTES OF A BEING THAT COULD HAVE DESIGNED AND CREATED THE WORLD OF NATURE

The nature and attributes of any being can best be known from what it creates. What a being creates is always a reflection of its nature and attributes.

Assume that the world of Nature was designed and created by a Being of some sort. What can you know about that Being from the attributes of the world of Nature?

The incredible diversity of the species of life in the world of Nature and the beneficial intricacy of the attributes of that life tells us that that Being is very creative, that it can imagine, that it can create what it imagines, that it knows the effect of what it creates, that it is intelligent.

The freedom of expression created by the harmonic conflict in the world of Nature that enables millions of species of life to successfully express their diverse and sometimes conflicting natures is the dominant effect of the incredible diversity of the species of life in the world of Nature. It is the harmony of the conflict in that world that creates that freedom. Without that harmony, the freedom of each species of life to express their conflicting natures could not exist.

From the universal freedom of expression being produced by the world of Nature, it can be concluded that the Being that created that world has a harmonic nature that gives every species of life that it creates the ability to fully express its nature.

The universal freedom and harmony being expressed by the mammoth array of life in the very competitive world of Nature is evidence that that Being has the ability to create freedom and harmony in any situation, for the world of Nature produces freedom and harmony in a sea of deadly conflict. The ultimate effect of the world of Nature is harmonic conflict that produces the freedom of every species to express its nature. The deadly conflict in the world of Nature does not prevent every species of life in that world from expressing its nature.

The freedom of every species of life in Nature to express its nature is preserved by the harmony produced by the attributes of the species of life in Nature. The world of Nature harmoniously preserves both the freedom and conflict of the diverse species of life in that world.

It is the freedom of the species of life in Nature to express their conflicting natures that the harmony in the world of Nature preserves. It is freedom that the world of Nature is preserving with the harmony of its conflict.

Freedom of expression is then very important to the Being that created the world of Nature and it is freedom of expression that you seek.

The energy of the world of Nature is its dominant attribute. It is from energy that everything in Nature is created and the energy of Nature has given every indication that it is limitless in its ability to become matter, species of life and create events. Only the energy of Nature is eternal in its existence. Everything else in Nature eventually ceases to exist and when the matter and life that the energy of Nature becomes, ceases to exist, the energy that became that matter and life emerges from that matter and life and reverts back to being exactly the same energy that it was before it became matter and life.

No portion of the energy in the world of Nature can be distinguished from any other portion of that energy, except by its immediate source, its magnitude, what it becomes and the effect it creates. This indistinguishable, formless attribute of that energy, its continued existence in the matter and life that it becomes and its formless emergence from that matter and life when that matter and life cease to exist, gives that energy an absolute oneness with itself and with everything it becomes, which is everything in the world of Nature, for everything in Nature is comprised of that energy.

From the attributes and effects of the energy in the world of Nature, it can be concluded that the pure formless, eternal energy of Nature, that is limitless in its ability to become matter and life, create effects and events, is one with itself and with everything it becomes and always returns to its primal state of pure formless limitless potential and indistinguishable oneness no matter what it becomes, is either the Being that imagined and created the world of Nature or is an expression of the essence of that Being, that it is a Being of pure endless energy that is capable of creating anything it imagines.

The absolute oneness of the energy that is the Being that created the world of Nature is the source of the incredible freedom and harmony that exists in the world of Nature, for absolute oneness is always dealing only with itself and would always give itself total freedom and would always harmonize with its own freedom.

Unless something can come from nothing, the existence of anything confirms that there is something that has always existed and if something has always existed, then its demonstrated survival makes it very likely that it will always continue to exist. It is easily concluded from the simple existence of the world of Nature that an attribute of the Being that is its source, is that it has always existed and will always exist, that its existence is eternal.

The constant evolution of the life in the world of Nature tells us that the Being that created the world of Nature continues to imagine and create different forms of life.

The matter and life in the world of Nature are always in a state of constant change and eventually always cease to exist as everything in Nature always reverts back to being the energy from which it was created. From this it can be concluded that whatever the Being that created the world of Nature creates, it never satisfies that Being, for everything in Nature eventually ceases to exist except the energy from which it came to be and that energy is either the Being that created that world or symbolizes that Being. From this it can be concluded that the absolute oneness and potential to create of that Being, not what it creates, must be that Being's source of greatest satisfaction. Its static existence in a state of absolute oneness and absolute potential to imagine and create must be the source of its greatest satisfaction.

From the absolute oneness expressed by the energy of the world of Nature and the incredible harmony and freedom that that energy creates in Nature, it can be concluded that absolute oneness is the dominant attribute of the Being that designed and created the world of Nature, for it is freedom and harmony that absolute oneness would always create in its necessity of always dealing with itself.

Absolute oneness could not create anything but freedom and harmony without contradicting itself.

Every species of life in Nature reproduces itself and its attributes in its offspring. From this it can be concluded that the Being that created the world of Nature, in some way, reproduces itself and its offspring have its attributes and in its absolute oneness it could experience through its offspring whatever its offspring experienced.

From the attributes of the world of Nature, it can be concluded that if a Being designed and created the world of Nature, it is an intelligent, creative, formless consciousness of pure energy, that is absolutely one with everything that exists, that the absolute oneness of that Being causes it to create freedom and harmony, that that Being has always existed, and is eternal in its existence, that it is the source of everything that exists, that through the constant evolution of the species of life in the world of Nature it continues to imagine new species of life and new beneficial attributes for the species of life in that world, that it is limitless in its ability to create what it imagines, that what it imagines and creates never satisfies that Being, that its source of absolute satisfaction is its absolute oneness and potential to create whatever it imagines.

How do human attributes compare with the attributes of the Being that we have imagined from the attributes of the world of Nature?

Humans are very special animals. There are other intelligent and creative animals, but only humans have the degree of intelligence and creativity that could have designed the world of Nature.

Humans are the only animal that has the ability to fully understand the cause and effect logic of the world of Nature. Humans are the only animal that can imagine other realities with different cause and effect logics and the intelligence to know the events that those realities would create. There is a distinct possibility that humans could be offspring of the Being that created the world of Nature and impeccable reasoning demands that that possibility be fully explored.

For what possible purpose would a Being with the attributes we have discovered from what it created, create a limited, competitive and dangerous world and then imprison fragments of itself in such a reality?

The stock answer to that question by those who believe that humans are some kind of offspring of the Being that created the world of Nature, has always been that humans are not capable of understanding the answer to that question, but the answer is very simple:

TO CREATE THE JOY OF OVERCOMING OR ESCAPING FROM SUCH A REALITY

THE CREATION OF JOY

Whenever a situation that you are experiencing becomes more positive, you experience joy. Whenever a situation that you are experiencing becomes less negative you experience joy. If you are dissatisfied and you experience satisfaction, you experience joy. If you are in despair and you experience hope, you experience joy. If you are suffering and your suffering ceases or diminishes, you experience joy. Whenever you experience something that is more positive, you will experience joy. Joy is your nature's most desired experience when you are not experiencing the absolute satisfaction of the absolute oneness and absolute potential of your primordial Beingness.

The limited, competitive, negative, dangerous world in which you struggle has the capacity to create more joy than any other kind of reality for a being that can overcome the negativity of that world or escape from that world. The reality in which you have imprisoned yourself is a study of potential negativity and would be a source of great joy to a being that could avoid or overcome that negativity or escape from such a reality and nothing could for long imprison a fragment of Beingness.

The root definition of the word *Allah*, that is the Muslim word for God, is the positive cancelling the negative. This is how joy is created.

In the absolute oneness of Beingness, it could experience the joy that such a reality could create if fragments of its Beingness became subject to that limited, competitive, negative and dangerous reality and those fragments proceeded to experience and then overcome the negative activity of that reality and finally escape in absolute joy from that negative reality to the absolute freedom of their true nature, and if the only escape from that reality appeared to be the non-existence produced by death, the joy of an escape would be even greater. Death is a very negative concept and everything in the world of Nature eventually ceases to exist.

The world of Nature has all of the attributes needed to create immense joy for such a Being, if it could become subject to such a reality, but this would be difficult to accomplish, for any fragment of Beingness would have all of the attributes of Beingness. It would be possessed of absolute intelligence, endless imagination and the freedom to create whatever it imagined. That freedom would have to be very much curtailed to imprison a fragment of Beingness in such a reality.

In the absolute oneness of Beingness with any fragment of itself, it could experience the joy being experienced by any fragment of itself when that fragment overcame any negative premise of that reality and when that fragment escaped from that reality to the absolute freedom of its nature, it would be the same as both the fragment of Beingness and Beingness in their absolute oneness, being newly born to their limitless potential. It would be a source of endless joy to Beingness if fragments of its Beingness continually escaped from such a reality.

The greater the dissatisfaction, suffering and despair that a fragment of Beingness experienced in such a reality, the greater its joy would be when it overcame that dissatisfaction, suffering and despair or simply escaped from such a reality. It would be impossible for the imprisonment of a fragment of Beingness in the limited, competitive and negative world of Nature not to create joy, for it would always escape from such a reality. Nothing could for long restrict a Being with the power to create whatever it imagines.

As a fragment of Beingness imprisoned in the cause and effect logic of the world of Nature and the logic of a world of humans, you are subject to experiencing the dissatisfaction, suffering and despair that such a reality creates so that you and Beingness can experience the joy of avoiding, overcoming and escaping dissatisfaction, suffering and despair to experience the absolute freedom of your Beingness.

How fulfilling is joy? Beethoven was one of the greatest composers that ever lived. His ninth, last and most famous symphony is comprised of four movements. The first three movements describe what Beethoven believed to be the three major modes of experiencing life. They are rural simplicity, urban frenzy and contemplative thought. In the fourth and final movement of that symphony, the first three movements are again introduced and each one is rejected by the fourth movement. The fourth movement then expresses what Beethoven believed to be the most satisfying and beautiful experience that we can have.

Beethoven entitled the fourth movement "Ode to Joy." It is regarded by many as the most beautifully uplifting movement in all of classical music. Beethoven considered joy to be the ultimate and most satisfying of all experiences. The fourth movement of Beethoven's ninth symphony expresses joy.

If this scenario seems implausible to you, then consider why people are willing to subject themselves to extreme danger to accomplish some difficult, but meaningless task, such as climbing a mountain in order to experience the satisfaction and joy of such an accomplishment? It is the joy of accomplishing what is difficult to accomplish. No other animal does this, only humans. We not only admire these people, to some extent we share in the joy of their accomplishment. It is the oneness of our nature that enables us to do this. Your Beingness is seeking to experience joy through you.

THE IMPRISONMENT OF BEINGNESS

If the Being that created the world of Nature desired to actually experience the limitations, conflicts, dissatisfaction and suffering that such a reality creates, so that it could experience the joy of overcoming them and finally the joy of escaping from such a reality to the absolute freedom of its nature, it would be necessary that a fragment of its Beingness be imprisoned in the cause and effect logic of that reality.

Beingness in its absolute oneness with every fragment of itself could experience whatever a fragment of its Beingness experienced in such a reality.

In the limitless imagination of Beingness and its absolute freedom to create whatever it imagined, there would be no limitation as to what Beingness could do to accomplish this.

If a fragment of Beingness was going to suffer so that it could experience the joy of escaping from that suffering, it would, in its absolute freedom, have to cause itself to suffer and it would have to cause itself to be unaware that it was causing itself to suffer. For an escape from suffering to create joy, it would have to be a real escape from real suffering. To simply knowingly cause yourself to suffer so that you could stop causing yourself to suffer would not create the joy of an escape from suffering. It would not be a real escape. An escape must overcome a real obstruction. In the absolute freedom of a fragment of Beingness, it would have to be creating the obstruction to its own escape.

To imprison a fragment of Beingness in a negative reality would require that the fragment of Beingness become totally unaware of its ability to create whatever it imagined. It would be necessary for the cause and effect logic of the reality into which it was born to control the creative ability of the fragment of Beingness and cause it to imprison itself in the limited and negative premises of that reality.

For a fragment of Beingness to suffer, it would have to be induced to unknowingly cause itself to suffer.

For a fragment of Beingness to fully experience the joy of escaping from a reality that creates suffering, the imprisonment of the fragment of Beingness in that reality would have to be complete and durable. The fragment of Beingness would have to be absolutely convinced that it was subject to the cause and effect logic of that reality to experience the dissatisfaction and suffering that the limiting and negative premises of such a reality naturally create.

The fragment of Beingness would have to be born into some species of life in the world of Nature. All of that life is by its nature subject to the cause and effect logic of the world of Nature and to the dissatisfaction and suffering that logic naturally produces. The most talented and versatile life in the world of Nature are animals.

It would be necessary for Beingness to create an animal with the intelligence and imagination that a fragment of Beingness would identify with when that animal matured, but had animal traits as an embryo, infant and child that would imprison a fragment of Beingness in that animal's instincts, physical attributes and expectations and in the cause and effect logic of that reality and Beingness created Homo sapiens and gave them the animal attributes that would accomplish this.

The Homo sapien animal, because of its monumental brain, is the most intelligent of all species of life in the world of Nature. Its intelligence is of such potential magnitude that, over time, it is able to understand much of the cause and effect logic of the elements in the world of Nature and its intelligence and memory of past events and situations enables it to predict many future events and to imagine tools and Beingness gave Homo sapiens a hand that is the most versatile physical tool possessed by any species of life, that enabled it to construct and use the tools it imagined. A fragment of Beingness would very much identify with such a talented animal when it matured, but it was first necessary to imprison the fragment of Beingness in that animal.

Imprisoning a fragment of Beingness in the attributes and attitude of an animal and in the cause and effect logic of the world of nature would be difficult to accomplish. Its absolute freedom to create what it imagined would have to be totally subjugated. The attention of the fragment of Beingness would have to be totally captured by the situation of the animal into which it was born and that situation had to be a state of absolute helplessness to disable the absolute freedom of a fragment of Beingness and that animal's helplessness and dependency on others to survive would have to persist for a very long period of time to totally subjugate the absolute freedom of a fragment of Beingness to create what it imagined.

During the period of gestation of a Homo sapien baby, like every animal, it is absolutely helpless in every respect. The attention of a fragment of Beingness born into a Homo sapien baby that is in its mother's womb would have no choice, but to focus all of its attention on the absolute helplessness of that baby, and believing that it was that baby be imprisoned in that baby's helplessness.

A fragment of Beingness born into a Homo sapien baby would be forced by its absolute identification with that animal and that animal's absolute helplessness to believe that it was absolutely helpless and the continued absolute and then extreme helplessness of that animal for many years after its birth would solidify its helplessness and imprison the fragment of Beingness in the absolute vulnerability of that helpless animal.

The period of time that a Homo sapien child is absolutely helpless to survive on its own is six or seven years and a Homo sapien child continues to be very dependent on its parents for survival until it is nine or ten years old.

Is there any evidence that the Homo sapien animal was designed to have a long period of gestation and a long and intensely helpless childhood that would imprison a fragment of Beingness in its animal attributes and attitude and thus in the cause and effect logic of the world of Nature, but would eventually develop the intelligence and creativity that a fragment of Beingness would identify with?

Homo sapiens are evolutionary freaks. They have a combination of the most extremely beneficial and the most extremely detrimental physical attributes that an animal can have, but they are attributes that would imprison a fragment of Beingness in that animal. No other animal has this combination of attributes and very, very few have any of these attributes. They are physical attributes that would imprison a fragment of Beingness in the helplessness of that animal and cause it to identify with that animal.

Perhaps the most detrimental attributes of animal can have in its struggle to survive in the world of Nature would be a long period of gestation and a long period of dependency on its mother for survival after its birth. The longer it takes a species of life in the world of Nature to survive on its own the more vulnerable that species is to extinction.

The intelligence of the Homo sapien brain, its ability to predict future events based on past events, to imagine useful tools and to understand the cause and effect logic of the world of Nature far exceeds that of any other animal and these are attributes that a fragment of Beingness would very much identify with.

The shorter the period of gestation of an animal, the more likely an offspring will be born and the shorter the time it takes an animal to be independent of its mother for survival, the more durable the species of animal will be.

The nine month gestation period of Homo sapiens is much longer than almost every other animal. Almost every other animal except Homo sapiens can survive on its own within three years after its birth and most can survive on their own in far less than three years, Homo sapiens are very helpless and dependent until they are seven years old and often very dependent on others until they are nine or ten.

The extremely long and absolutely helpless dependency of humans on their parents would be catastrophic to any other species of animal, but is needed to imprison a fragment of Beingness in the attributes and attitude of that animal.

It is not difficult to perceive that Homo sapiens have purposely been given animal attributes that would be very detrimental to the survival of any other animal, but are absolutely necessary to imprison a fragment of Beingness in that animal.

Many humans have concluded that humans have two distinct natures. One is a predatory, fearful, practical, violent animal nature and the other is a highly creative and harmonic nature.

Beingness has caused Homo sapiens to have all of the animal attributes needed to imprison a fragment of Beingness in their attributes and in the cause and effect logic of the limited and negative world of Nature. The imprisonment is very complete; the prison is very secure and durable.

Now you need to understand how you create, attract and affect events.

HOW YOUR EXPECTATIONS CREATE, ATTRACT AND AFFECT EVENTS

You have several ways that you create, attract and affect the events of your life. You can create and affect an event by using the cause and effect logic of the world in which you are imprisoned. Virtually everyone believes that this is how all events are created and affected. The fact is that the expectations of your core attitude determine all of the events of your life.

There is no question that your expectations can have a dramatic effect on the health of your body (the placebo effect) and there is more than enough evidence that your expectations can directly affect the elements that make up the world of Nature, for you to conclude that your expectations could have far more effect on the events of your life than you have ever imagined.

Your core attitude is the source of all of your expectations. Your core attitude is the source of your personal logic. Your core attitude is always certain of the kind of events you will experience and it attracts events and affects the circumstances of those events to make them match your core attitude's positive or negative expectations.

Your core attitude can be positive or negative and any degree of positive or negative, but the reality in which you are imprisoned does not promote extremely positive core attitudes. An extremely positive core attitude is very rare.

Your core attitude is always experiencing the positive or negative flavor of the events it is expecting, attracting and affecting without knowing exactly what those events will be, only their positive or negative flavor.

An extremely negative core attitude is constantly attracting detrimental events and circumstances and an extremely positive core attitude is constantly attracting beneficial events and circumstances.

There will always be particular kinds of events that you are more positive or negative about and this will directly affect your success or failure regarding those activities. It is the positive or negative expectation of your core attitude that creates, attracts and repels events.

The expectations of your core attitude are attracting all of the events in your life and the circumstances of those events that make them positive or negative.

If you have negative expectations, you will attract negative events or negative circumstances for positive events that will convert a positive event into a negative event. If you have positive expectations, you will attract positive events or positive circumstances for negative events that will convert a negative event into a positive event. You will not know exactly what those events and circumstances will be, but they will always be a perfect match with your attitude's level of negativity or positiveness regarding the future.

Who then is deciding what event you should experience to reflect what your core attitude is expecting?

Your Beingness creates or attracts whatever kind of event that your core attitude is expecting.

Your core attitude is the prison from which you must escape. The most powerful attribute of every core attitude is that it is always imprisoned by the fear that the reality in which you are imprisoned naturally produces.

Your core attitude controls the positive or negative flavor of the events you create, attract or repel. Your core attitude simply causes your Beingness to create, attract or repel the events and the circumstances needed to reflect the negative or positive flavor of your core attitude.

Your core attitude does not have to always create events to reflect your core attitude. It can attract an event or change the circumstances of an event that will affect the positive or negative flavor of the event

There are more than enough circumstances and events being created by others to match whatever flavored event that your attitude is demanding that you experience, but the positive and negative tone of the period of time in which you live very much determines the overall flavor of the events available for your attitude to attract and create.

Does this all seem to be terribly improbably to you? It is not a new concept that an individual's attitude is very important as regards to the quality of the events that they create and experience.

It can be observed that the attitude of some people tends to expect positive events and circumstances and they seem to experience more positive events and circumstances and they are deemed to be lucky.

It can also be observed that the attitude of some people tends to expect negative events and circumstances and they seem to experience more negative events and circumstances and they are deemed to be unlucky.

Is it not strange to you that people very seldom ever change their attitude, no matter now twisted or illogical it may seem to be to you? Shouldn't the events they experience change their attitude? They never change their attitude because the events that they experience always validate whatever attitude they have.

How rare is it to observe a person change their attitude? Everyone's attitude always becomes more and more entrenched because every attitude always validates itself. The older a person becomes the more entrenched their attitude becomes. This is more easily observed in others if their attitude is radically different than your attitude, for the events and circumstances that their attitude attracts will be very different from the events and circumstances that your attitude attracts.

It is easily observed that the positive or negative flavor of the events of everyone's life always have an absolute regularity to them. Shouldn't the luck of the draw, that is the law of probabilities, create a greater variety of good and bad events for each person? It doesn't because it is not probabilities that create the events being experienced by humans. It is their core attitudes.

It is easily observed that people of different economic and social status have very different attitudes that produce very different events in their lives – events that match their attitude, which makes it difficult for people to change their economic and social status.

It is easy to conclude that the cause and effect logic of the world in which you struggle created the events and circumstances you have experienced and thus created your attitude. It is difficult to conclude otherwise, for you are totally unaware of the freedom of your Beingness to create, attract, repel and affect events.

Your attitude is your underlying expectations of the positive or negative events you will experience. You are constantly experiencing, in the present moment, with your attitude, the events that your attitude expects and then attracts or causes you to create.

Everyone's attitude is totally dominated by the events their attitude has caused them to attract, affect and experience in the past. The seeming logic of past events always becomes the prison from which you must escape.

The precise effect of a human expectation is impossible to measure, for the intensity, quality and effect of a human expectation cannot be measured except by its effect, just as a placebo does not always create the placebo effect. You are in a very delicate, but messy situation and you agreed to be in the situation that you are in.

Knowing the truth of your nature will not set you free. Only the positivity of your attitude can set you free and your attitude is totally content with itself. Why wouldn't it be? It has always been correct in its expectations. It causes you to create or it attracts what it expects. The events of your life and the lives of many others will always oppose having a more positive attitude. You are imprisoned in a very negative reality.

There is absolutely no doubt that a human expectation can cause an absolutely ordinary event (a placebo) to have an extremely beneficial effect on a human body. The placebo effect has endlessly demonstrated the ability of human expectations to do this. There is also little doubt that a human expectation can cause an absolutely ordinary event (a nocebo) to have an extremely detrimental effect on a human body. The nocebo effect has demonstrated this many, many times.

There is more than enough evidence of the ability of human expectations (attitude) to affect events and the elements in Nature to conclude that human expectations could be affecting all of the events that humans experience far more than you have ever imagined.

WHERE YOU GOT YOUR
CORE ATITUDE

You were both induced and driven by the attitudes and behavior of those who raised you to have the same attitude and behavior that they had, that creates and attracts the same positive or negative tone of events that their attitudes caused them to experience and caused you to also experience or observe during your childhood when your Beingness was unable to attract or create events because of its intense focus on the helplessness of the animal child it inhabited.

Your core attitude is absolutely certain that you will continue to experience the same kind of events that those who raised you caused you to experience and observe.

Your core attitude is your expectation as to what kind of events the world in which you struggle will cause you to experience. It is the kind of event that your attitude expects that is actually creating, attracting and affecting the events that you experience. Your attitude is in effect the sum total of your personal logic regarding the reality in which you struggle and that logic is controlling all the events of your life.

Most of your present attitude was created during the period in your childhood and youth when others were creating most of the events in your life.

Your helplessness as an infant and as a child and your very dependent need for others to take care of you until you were nine or ten years old turned the creation of most of the events of your life over to the attitude of others and their attitudes created the significant events of your childhood and those events validated their attitudes and caused you to embrace the same or a similar attitude.

The effect of the attitudes of those who raised you, on the events their attitudes caused you to experience or observe as a child, molded your present attitude. In a sense, it was their gift to you, for they believed that their attitude was absolutely the best attitude to have. Everyone believes that their attitude is the best attitude to have because everyone's attitude is always validated by the events that they experience or do not experience.

Your present attitude is always some variation of the attitudes of those who raised you. The apple does not fall far from the tree. Your attitude can change for the better or worse and with a corresponding effect on the events of your life, but it is difficult to change an attitude that is constantly validating itself, for it is not rational to change an attitude that is constantly validating itself, no matter how negative it is, and every attitude always validates itself. Increasing your knowledge of the cause and effect logic of the world in which you are imprisoned will always improve your attitude to some extent, but will not enable you to escape the prison that is your present core attitude.

Your attitude, by virtue of the events that you were taught to expect by your parents, family, or those who raised you, and by the events that the attitudes of those people caused you to experience or observe while you were imprisoned in your helpless and very dependent childhood can be a conglomeration of the attitudes of those people, but people in the same family, culture and social strata tend to have very similar attitudes. Your attitude will tend to be the attitude of the prominent person or persons in your childhood.

Your animal nature is very practical. Its brain remembers everything and always expects the future to be a replica of the past and constantly advises you of this with its behavior and its dialogue with you. Your animal brain is always the champion of your attitude no matter what your attitude is. Your animal brain is the foremost expert as to the kind of event that your attitude produces.

Because of the imprisonment of your Beingness, first in helplessness and then in various degrees of dependency while your animal body matured to its independence, you were forced to be subject to the attitudes of those who raised you and to the events their attitudes caused you to experience and observe. You learned what to expect from those who raised you and this became your attitude. This became your personal logic and your Beingness will always cause what you experience to verify the validity of your personal logic.

The world is filled with a multitude of different attitudes. Beingness obviously desired to experience the world in which you are imprisoned from every conceivable attitude, all of which produce a different flavor of joy when they are overcome. Every stage of your life from youth, adulthood, parenthood, middle age, and old age presents different situations for your attitude to create or attract events to match whatever your attitude is. Being male or female promotes different attitudes and events. Different races, countries and climates create different attitudes and events.

It is your imprisoned Beingness that creates your world. Your attitude can be confident, fearful, careful, bold, timid, cooperative, defensive, etc., and any degree of those attitudes. Any attitude you embrace, your Beingness will always validate with the events you experience.

Beingness willingly pays the price of experiencing dissatisfaction, suffering and despair to experience the joy of overcoming or escaping from dissatisfaction, suffering and despair.

You believe that the reality in which you struggle created your attitude, not that your attitude is directing through your Beingness how that reality will respond to you, but it is your attitude that is creating your world. Your attitude is your personal logic as to how the world will respond to you and your attitude is always right.

If we are taught, usually by our parents, to have a particular attitude, how is it that a family can produce individual members with very different attitudes?

The Homo sapien animal, like every animal, produces offspring with a variety of temperaments.

The instinctual temperament of a Homo sapien animal can be aggressive, violent, timid, careful and any variation of those temperaments. Any animal biologist will confirm that every individual animal has its own distinct temperament no matter what species it may be.

The temperament of the animal into which a fragment of Beingness is born very much influences its behavioral response to the kind of events that your core attitude will produce.

You will discover that the behavior of your animal nature has the ability, if you choreograph it, to improve the positiveness of your attitude and the events your attitude causes your Beingness to create and attract.

Your animal nature will never even suspect that your attitude, which you were trained to have, is creating, attracting and affecting all of the events of your life, but it quickly learns that the past always repeats itself. The past always repeats itself because your attitude is creating, attracting, affecting and controlling every event in your life with its positive and negative expectations.

Your animal brain, by keeping track of the past, knows what to expect from the future and thus how to get ready for the future with its behavior and it constantly advises you of this with its incessant dialogue with you.

If Beingness desired to experience the joy of escaping from every possible attitude, the temperament of the animal that a fragment of Beingness inhabits would be a rich source of diverse responses to the same attitude.

Your animal nature's behavior always reveals what kind of event that your attitude is expecting and the more significant the event, the more its behavior will reveal your attitude. Both your attitude and your behavior are products of your underlying expectations regarding the events you will experience.

When you observed, as a child, an event being experienced by whoever raised you; there was an overwhelming inducement for you to expect the same kind of event from the same situation.

Why would you doubt the validity of an expectation that had been proven to be valid before your very eyes? This is how you got your attitude.

It was impossible for you to reject the attitudes of those who created the events of your childhood with their attitude and to reject their behavior that matched their attitude.

As a child, you were first absolutely helpless and then you were very dependent on others as to the events of your life. Others created with their attitude the events of your life and those events trained you to have the same attitude. Your attitude at some point began creating, attracting and affecting the events of your life and those events of course validated your attitude.

If everyone's attitude is creating the events of their life and if they had no control of what their attitude would be, then Christ's admonishment of *"Judge not"* is totally understandable.

You are imprisoned by the attitude that you were taught to have and no facts can ever release you from the prison of that attitude, for the facts that you encounter have already and will continue to validate the expectations of your present attitude.

Your animal brain is the greatest promoter of your present attitude, for your present attitude has been validated by all of the events that you have experienced during your entire life and those events are indelibly recorded in your animal brain for future reference. Your animal nature is constantly reminding you with its behavior and incessant dialogue with you of what your attitude is and that it should not change.

Your animal nature is certain that the past will always repeat itself and its constant dialogue with you is constantly fortifying the expectations of your present attitude that is both attracting and affecting all of the events of your life.

Your animal nature is very practical. It always believes that the past will repeat itself and as long as it is controlling your attitude with its behavior and its dialogue with you, the past will always repeat itself, many times to your consternation if you have a very negative attitude. Your animal nature will never stop advising you with its behavior and its continuous dialogue with you, but you can change your attitude and attract events that contradict the past and your animal nature will eventually change its expectations when the events created by your new attitude continually contradict your previous attitude. Your animal nature is very practical.

Your animal nature, and its intelligence regarding what events to expect, will always oppose any attempt to change your attitude. You can escape from the tyranny of your present attitude, but it is very difficult to do, for all of the events of your life have validated your present attitude.

CHANGING YOUR ATTITUDE

Your core attitude is simply what you expect the positive or negative flavor of the future events of your life will be. It is very difficult for anyone to change their attitude, because their present attitude has created all of the events in their life and those events have totally validated the correctness of their attitude in predicting the positive or negative flavor of the events they have experienced.

Since every attitude always validates itself, you will have to cause your attitude to be more positive to attract more positive events into your life.

For you to desire to change your attitude you will have to conclude that your present attitude is creating and attracting detrimental events into your life or is repelling positive events. Either can be true. A negative attitude attracts detrimental events and repels positive events and causes you to create detrimental events rather than positive events.

You are perfectly happy with your present attitude. Why wouldn't you be? Your present attitude has proven that it knows exactly what kind of events you will experience. Your attitude does know what kind of events to expect. It is unknowingly causing your Beingness to create those events and it will continue to do this no matter what you do, for you cannot cease having an attitude and the expectations of your attitude cannot cease causing the events you experience to match its expectations, but you can change your attitude to one that expects and thus attracts more positive events.

The only absolutely, indisputable scientific fact that your expectations can directly create an event is the placebo effect. The placebo effect has endlessly been validated to be able to cause humans to heal their body with the power of their expectations. However, the facts supporting the direct effect of human expectations on the purity of water, changing the nature of sunlight, controlling the movement of objects and directing the energy in Nature are more than substantial.

There are enough facts for anyone to at least suspect that their attitude, that is a positive or negative distillation of all of their expectations, could be attracting and affecting more of the events of their life than they realize.

You need to change your attitude to a more positive attitude for you to experience more positive events in your life. Your animal nature will always oppose any change in your attitude with its endless dialogue and with its behavior, which will always support the validity of your present attitude. Your animal nature knows exactly what kind of event that your present attitude expects. It has been observing and recording in its animal brain all of the events that your attitude has attracted into your entire life and knows that your attitude has always been correct in the kind of event it expects.

Your animal brain is the foremost expert in the world as to what your attitude expects for it always expects the past to constantly repeat itself. Your animal brain has recorded all of the events that your attitude has already attracted and affected. Your animal nature is very comfortable with your present attitude no matter how negative it is, because it has always been right in its expectations. Of course it has. It is causing your Beingness to create or attract what it is expecting.

Your animal brain is totally aware of what your attitude is. The behavior of your animal nature will always tell you what kind of event that your attitude is expecting and it will always be correct.

All of your physical routines are confirming some element of your attitude. You must study your routines to discover what part of your attitude they are supporting and change them to more positive routines.

Your animal brain is constantly telling you what to expect based on the kind of events that your attitude has created and attracted in the past. It knows exactly the kinds of events that your attitude always attracts or causes you to create, but it does not know that it is your attitude that is causing your Beingness to create and attract those events. It just knows that the past always repeats itself.

As unlikely as it may seem, the behavior of your animal nature that will always support your imprisonment in your present attitude is the key to your escape from your present attitude to a more positive attitude.

You must oppose the directives of your animal brain and behave more positively regarding every situation you are in, but you cannot successfully bully your present attitude. It is controlling the absolute freedom of your Beingness to attract or repel any event or cause you to create any event. If you drive your present attitude into intense fear with your behavior, it will create what it fears to your detriment.

You must edge up to a more positive attitude incrementally. It can be done a little at a time.

Understand that behavior is very important to an animal. Animals learn by watching the behavior of other animals like them and communicate with other animals with their behavior. Words can be very deceiving. Actions always speak louder than words for an animal.

Be aware that the first communications between your animal nature and your Beingness was when your animal nature was only a very small child and could only communicate what it was expecting with its behavior. It had not yet learned how to communicate verbally.

Its behavior is still your animal nature's most direct way of communicating what it is expecting and you can control the behavior of your animal nature to express more positive expectations and your Beingness will respond by creating more positive events in your life.

Seems very unlikely, doesn't it, but it is not difficult to find out if it will work. Just start acting more positively about everything and discover the effect on your life.

A person's behavior reveals more about that person's attitude than anything else. Each of us is portraying in our behavior the attitude that has imprisoned us.

As Shakespeare said *"All the world is a stage and all the men and women merely players."* You are very accurately portraying the character that is your attitude, which is the character you were taught to portray by whoever raised you. You need to improve the attitude of the character you are portraying and this can be accomplished by changing your behavior.

Actors must be very aware of the attitude of the character that they are portraying, for the art of acting is to accurately portray the underlying attitude of that character.

Words alone cannot fully communicate an attitude. The art of acting is to deliver words in the manner and with the physical behavior that reveals the attitude of the character that said the words. The art of acting is to cause your physical behavior, which includes your voice, gestures and demeanor to reflect the underlying attitude of the character being portrayed. You must pretend with your animal behavior that you are expecting positive events.

You must begin to act more positively to every situation. How effective is this?

Stage actors, after playing a particularly strong character for an extended period of time (sometimes twice a day), have found that the attitude of the character that they are portraying has affected their personal attitude, sometimes beneficially and sometimes detrimentally depending on the attitude of the character they are portraying.

Physically portraying a different attitude will cause you to experience that attitude to some degree and that experience will weaken your present attitude and will eventually change your attitude if you continue to physically portray that attitude.

I have always been drawn to the special magic of the live theater and I was fortunate to personally know a very successful stage actress, who at the very peak of her career abruptly ceased acting entirely and confided to her close friends that acting was having a detrimental effect on her personal attitude and her life. I saw her perform in the last play she ever did. With the consummate skill of a seasoned and talented actress, she was portraying a disturbed unhappy woman, a person that you would not want to be in real life. It was the kind of role that had driven the success of her career, but portraying such an attitude had injured her personal attitude.

Movie actors have found that they will portray the attitude of a character better if they constantly maintain that character's attitude even when they are not shooting a scene. Some directors will demand that everyone, during the entire time that a movie is being shot, if the moving is being shot at a special location, respond to an especially important actor in the movie as if that actor is the person that the actor is portraying in the movie. This has proven to be very effective in enhancing the quality of an actor's performance. The actor can more deeply experience the attitude they are portraying. They are being treated like the person they are portraying, which enhances their ability to portray the attitude of that person.

You must physically portray the attitude of a person that is expecting positive events in order to create and attract positive events into your life. Changing your attitude is a full time job. It requires imagination, patience, persistence and at times some degree of courage.

The behavior of your animal nature is always a perfect reflection of your attitude. Your animal nature is constantly fortifying the expectations of your attitude with its behavior, but you can control the behavior of your animal nature and the behavior of your animal nature can change your attitude, it is only necessary that you, like an actor playing a part, cause your animal nature to behave like your attitude is more positive. This will cause your attitude to become more positive and cause your Beingness to create and attract more positive events. To change your attitude, you must cause the behavior of your animal nature to respond more positively to everything. You must cause your animal nature to make positive physical gestures regarding every situation.

It will be necessary for you to edge up to and gradually assume the behavior that will set you free. Fear is the most powerful and detrimental attribute of your attitude. If your new behavior causes you to experience fear, you are very close to creating what you fear. Fear has appeared to be a very beneficial attitude many times in your life. It is difficult to discard what seems to have been beneficial in preventing your dissatisfaction and suffering from increasing. Fear is always a dominant attribute of every attitude and the primary attribute of a negative attitude. You now have an animal attitude. Everyone does. An animal always expects the past to repeat itself.

Every positive event causes you to experience joy. A positive expectation of your core attitude is the equivalent of a positive event, because it will always attract a positive event.

You need to cause your core attitude to expect positive events.

Your core attitude is always experiencing, in the present moment, the positive or negative tone of the events it will attract or affect. Using the power of your Beingness, your core attitude creates, attracts and affects events with its expectations. Your core attitude is what you have been induced to have by those who raised you.

No matter what Beingness imagines and creates, it always resolves itself into joy.

For a more positive attitude to become effective in your life, it must be embraced by every attribute of your nature. It must be embraced by your desire, intent, intelligence, and imagination, but to be effective it must be reflected in your behavior. It is your intention that is the catalyst of change, but it is only unbending intent that can create the attitude that will set you free. You will know when you have embraced a more positive attitude. It will feel good. You will be experiencing the joy that the validation of your new attitude will produce. The effects of a more positive attitude on the events of your life will then validate the joy you are experiencing. The more positive your attitude becomes, the greater your satisfaction and joy will be.

The part of your present attitude that must be overcome first is your fear. It is always your most formidable foe.

To begin changing your attitude, it is necessary that your intelligence, at the very least, accept that there is some possibility that your attitude could be creating, attracting and affecting more of the events in your life than you realize.

If your attitude is creating your world, then envy, anger, revenge, hatred, violence and greed are all useless responses to a world that your attitude is creating. Your attitude is your only enemy.

It is your attitude that must change for you to experience the greatest satisfaction and joy that the reality in which you have imprisoned yourself can provide and the least suffering that it will cause you to experience. There are many levels of positive attitude that you can achieve.

Your present attitude is creating your present level of satisfaction, dissatisfaction, joy and suffering. You need to embrace an attitude that will create greater satisfaction and joy in your life.

This is not an easy task. It was not intended to be easy for you to escape the prison that is your present attitude, for the more difficult that it is to escape, the more joy that your escape will cause you to experience.

The past will always validate your present attitude. Your attitude, like your animal nature, is always living in the past and is constantly causing your Beingness to recreate the past.

Your animal nature's intelligence will be a very vocal witness to the fact that your present attitude has been verified as valid by all of the events of your life as well as the lives of many others and will always oppose any change in your attitude. Your animal nature is very practical. It is well aware of what kind of action has best coped with the situations you have had to contend with in the past. Your animal nature cannot begin to change its expectations until your attitude begins to create and attract more than the usual beneficial events.

There can be no hard evidence that changing your attitude will change the events that you experience. Scientific verification is only available regarding the cause and effect logic of the world in which your attitude has imprisoned you and it is that logic that your new attitude will contradict and overcome.

You are imprisoned by your attitude. Very few people ever change their attitude. It is impossible for facts to change your attitude, for they will always validate whatever attitude you already have. It is a circular prison.

You do not change your attitude in order to become a better, more considerate person. You are not the cause of the dissatisfaction and suffering of others. Like you, they are also creating with their attitude the world that they are experiencing. You change your attitude in order to experience greater satisfaction and joy in your life, but your attitude when it produces more positive events can have a positive effect on the attitude of others.

Your escape will not be verifiable to others. The events that your new attitude attracts, modifies or causes you to create will all be probable events of the reality in which you struggle. Your attitude simply attracts to you people, circumstances and events that validate your new attitude and there are plenty of people, events and circumstances in the world in which you struggle to validate any positive attitude that you will be able to embrace, just as there are plenty of people, events and circumstances to validate any negative attitude you may have.

Expecting positive events is a positive attitude's full time job; just as worrying is the full time job of a negative attitude.

It is not necessary to imagine and experience a particular beneficial event to create a beneficial event when you have a positive attitude. A positive attitude simply expects beneficial events without knowing what those events will be. Your Beingness will create and attract the appropriate event to match your attitude.

How knowledgeable you are will always have a positive effect on your attitude. Many, many events can be intellectually predicted from the cause and effect logic of the world in which you struggle. The more events that you can intellectually predict the more positive your attitude will be and the more positive the events your attitude creates and attracts will be. Any kind of education creates a more positive attitude and thus more positive events in your life, but it will not give you a pure understanding of the situation you are in.

Do not act positively in the face of intense fear, only in the face of discomfort. Fear is an attitude that must first be diminished and then eliminated.

To change your attitude your actions regarding your problems must be more positive. You can cause yourself to act more positively when you are not positive about a situation. This is how you make your core attitude more positive. This will have a positive effect on your attitude, but if this causes you to experience intense fear rather than just discomfort, you are only promoting your negative attitude with your positive actions.

Acting as if you are positive in some way will always have a beneficial effect on your attitude, but start by acting positively about unimportant matters and work your way up to more important matters.

Anything that prevents you from experiencing a negative expectation is beneficial to your developing more positive expectations. To change your attitude that has been constantly validated by the events of your life and the lives of many others demands extreme and persistent effort from every point of view. It will demand your constant attention over a period of time, just as a weight lifter must persistently oppose gravity to become stronger. You need to overcome the gravity of your present attitude.

What positive attitude would be easiest to achieve and maintain? It would seem that the attitude that you are safe from harm would be the easiest positive attitude to assume. Most people have experienced being safe on numerous occasions. That you will get what you need is probably the next easiest positive attitude to assume. These are the attitudes that most religions promote as the effect of their precepts and beliefs. Following the precepts and beliefs of a particular religion does improve the attitude of many people and improve the events that their attitudes create. Being safe and getting what you need are not the most beneficial attitudes, but are better than many other attitudes. From these attitudes it would be easier to develop an even more positive attitude.

Assuming a more positive attitude in the face of a lifetime of events that have validated your present attitude is very difficult. Your Beingness intended it to be difficult. The greater the difficulty, the greater the joy of accomplishment.

MORE ABOUT CHANGING YOUR ATTITUDE BY CHANGING YOUR BEHAVIOR

That your attitude is creating and attracting all of the events of your life is difficult enough to embrace. That the behavior of your animal nature directly affects the expectations of your attitude and the events that it causes your Beingness to create and attract seems so unlikely that it is hard to believe that this is possible; but your animal nature has dominated your attitude ever since you were born into that animal. This is how you were imprisoned in the reality in which you struggle.

As unlikely as it may seem to be, the physical behavior of your animal nature is far and away the most effective way of directing the creative power of your Beingness to create or attract positive events.

How could simply causing the behavior of your animal nature to be more positive regarding any situation you may be in, possibly enhance the positive expectations of your core attitude and thus cause it to create or attract a more positive outcome to that situation? It was the animal behavior of whoever raised you that originally told your core attitude what to expect.

The first humans were not raised by humans. They were raised by the Homo sapien animal that gave them birth and by its family and tribe. The first humans were taught to have a totally animal attitude and the first humans then taught their offspring to have their animal attitude. The attitude of the first humans learned what to expect by observing the behavior of the animals that raised them. Your attitude learned what to expect from the behavior of whoever raised you, just as the first humans did. It was the attitude of those who raised you that created and attracted the events that they experienced and caused you to experience. It was the animal attitude of the Homo sapien animal that created the events that the first humans experienced and taught the first humans to have a totally animal attitude.

What exactly is an animal attitude? It is a combination of the instincts of the animal and its memory of the events it has observed or experienced. The instinctual attitude of an animal regarding any situation is a direct reflection of the ability of its physical attributes to successfully handle the situation. An animal brain remembers prior events that it has experienced and this affects its response to any situation based on the outcome of those prior events.

The Homo sapien brain has a staggering capacity to remember prior events and this very much affects how it will respond to every situation it may encounter. The past is very important to the Homo sapien brain in determining what to expect and how to respond to any situation.

The animal attitude of the Homo sapien animal that humans inhabit relies not only on its instincts to handle a situation; it also relies on the outcome of prior event to determine its best response to any situation. Your animal nature's brain is convinced that the past will repeat itself and its behavior will always reflect that expectation.

The animal attributes of the Homo sapien animal (except for its monumental brain) are not impressive. It does not have great size, speed or strength and it has no physical weapons such as predatory claws or teeth. Nor does it have fur to protect its body from injury and weather and the primordial jungle in which Homo sapiens originally lived was a very dangerous place for such a physically defenseless animal. There were many predators with physical attributes that were far more impressive than the physical attributes of the Homo sapien animal.

This made fear a very valuable attitude for the Homo sapien animal to have and cultivate, but fear if it is intense enough, will cause the Beingness of humans to attract what is feared. Fear can be a very dangerous attitude for a human.

Fear is the foundation of the prison from which a fragment of Beingness born into a Homo sapien animal must escape.

The intense fear of your core attitude is always a self-fulfilling prophesy. Fear, like any human attitude, creates and attracts the event it is expecting.

If your core attitude is induced to create or attract a positive event, the positiveness of your overall expectations will be enhanced regarding all future situations. Every human attitude feeds on itself.

The attributes of your Beingness are exactly the same as they were when its power to create was imprisoned in your present core attitude.

Your Beingness is always exercising its power to create, attract and affect events; but now that power is being used to create, attract and affect events that match the positive or negative expectations of your present core attitude.

The attributes of your Beingness cannot change, but you can change what your Beingness creates and attracts by simply changing your behavior.

Your Beingness was imprisoned in your present attitude and in the events that attitude naturally creates and attracts, by first observing, as a child, the behavior of the humans that raised you, as their animal behavior responded to a multitude of situations and then by observing that their animal behavior always very accurately predicted the event that they experienced from those situations, events that you also many times experienced because they were, in your helplessness as a child, also creating the events of your life.

The behavior of your animal nature is constantly reminding your attitude of the kind of event to expect from every situation based on your past. Your animal brain does not know that your attitude is controlling the events of your life. You can control the physical behavior of your animal nature and cause it to send your Beingness more positive messages with its behavior and your Beingness will respond positively to those messages. You are well aware of the kind of animal behavior that is expecting a positive event and the kind of animal behavior that is expecting a negative event. Everyone has experienced both positive and negative events.

Your animal brain is now directing the behavior of your animal nature in every situation you are in. That behavior is based on the negative or positive flavor of the events that your present attitude has attracted into your life. Your animal brain knows exactly the kind of events to expect, for it has recorded all of the events of your life and it always expects the past to repeat itself because it always has.

Your brain's incessant dialogue with you constantly reminds your attitude of what kind of event it should expect and tells you how your animal nature's behavior should prepare for that event. This always reinforces the kind of event that your attitude is already expecting and, of course, will then cause your Beingness to create or attract to match its expectations.

Your attitude is imprisoned in the cause and effect logic of the reality in which you struggle and in the limitations and fears that you were taught to have.

Your animal brain has another activity that is very detrimental to the health of your attitude. If you have a negative attitude, your animal brain will continually review the negative possibilities of every situation. It will worry. This is your animal nature's behavioral response to a very negative core attitude.

You can force your behavior to be more positive regarding a situation, but you cannot stop your animal brain from worrying. However, you can shut your brain down. This is very difficult to accomplish and sustain, for it requires a state of meditation, but keeping your brain occupied with other matters can also prevent it from worrying and negatively influencing your attitude.

Your core attitude is fully aware that your animal nature's behavior always very accurately predicts the events that you will experience. Your animal nature knows that the past will always repeat itself, because it always has and its brain has recorded the past for future reference.

Your animal baby-child nature that your Beingness was forced to embrace when it was born into a helpless Homo sapien baby, imprisoned your Beingness in its helplessness and then into absolutely trusting the animal behavior of those who raised it, to tell it what to expect. That trust still exists and you can cause your animal nature to behave in any way and its behavior will affect the expectations of your core attitude.

You can choreograph the behavior of your animal nature to be positive or just more positive if acting too positive increases the negative possibilities of a situation and would cause your core attitude to experience greater fear, which can, if the fear is intense enough, cause your attitude to attract what it fears. You cannot successfully bully your present core attitude, but you can push it with your behavior.

You can cause your behavior to respond positively or more positively to a situation and this will cause your core attitude to become more positive regarding that situation and to attract positive events regarding that situation.

Your core attitude is not always influenced by probabilities. An extremely negative attitude can convert even the best situation into a disaster. You may have observed this in the events that some humans create or attract.

Your core attitude is the product of your absolute trust in the expectations of those who raised you. Their behavior told your attitude what to expect. You got your core attitude from the attitude of those who raised you. They gave you their core attitude with all of its doubts and fears.

Your animal nature, expressing your expectations with its behavior, is always expressing the expectations of your core attitude and by doing so is telling your core attitude not to change.

It is not rational to believe that your attitude as regards any situation, that you may find yourself in, can make that situation turn out to be either positive or negative. Nor is it rational to believe that your behavior can change your attitude and cause it to attract positive events. The attributes, logic, power and response of your Beingness are not rational to your animal logic. Your animal nature will never fully accept the absolute freedom of your Beingness, but you can take control of your animal nature and cause its behavior to begin directing your attitude to be more positive and your attitude will respond to those directions by attracting more positive events.

It was the absolute trust of your forgotten child nature, in the animal behavior of whoever raised you, to always accurately predict future events that imprisoned you in your core attitude. Your child nature is still alive in your attitude and it will still respond to the negative or positive behavior of your animal nature and attract events that match that behavior.

A very detrimental negative behavior of your animal nature is the incessant worrying of its animal brain. This is the bedrock support of your animal nature to a negative attitude.

If you have a very negative core attitude, your animal brain will continually revisit every situation that you are in and all of the detrimental possibilities of those situations. This always increases the propensity of your core attitude to attract detrimental events, but you have the ability to shut down the dialogue of your animal brain.

You either know how to do this or you can learn how to do this by attempting to do it. You should review a bad situation only to determine if the situation has changed `and would benefit from an even more positive behavior.

It is difficult enough to have to deal with the negativity of your own core attitude. You must also avoid people with negative core attitudes. They will always want to advise you regarding any situation. They always believe it is very wise to figure out how many ways that a situation can go wrong. They never intend to injure you, but they always will. You need to view everything from a new more positive perspective.

The most beneficial and also the most detrimental attribute of every core attitude is that it always feeds on itself. Left alone, it will never change but when your attitude begins to attract positive events it will continue to attract positive events.

The core attitude that a fragment of Beingness is trained to have by those who raised it, will continue to create and attract the same positive or negative flavored events until the behavior of its animal nature tells it to do otherwise. Your animal behavior will always expect the past to repeat itself. Every core attitude is always being validated as being absolutely correct in its expectations by attracting the kind of events it expects. It always validates itself no matter how negative or positive it might be and your animal brain is keeping score. The expectations of your core attitude always prove to be correct. They can never be wrong. They are attracting whatever they are expecting and your animal nature with its physical behavior and dialogue with you is constantly agreeing with the expectations of your core attitude. Why would you change an attitude that always proves to be correct and you don't change it.

Only a pure understanding of who you really are, why you are in the situation you are in and how you got into that situation will enable you to exercise the freedom of your Beingness.

If a core attitude expects a beneficial event, it will attract a beneficial event. When it has attracted a beneficial event, it is then always more likely to attract another beneficial event. It always feeds on itself.

It is universally accepted that success breeds success. This phenomenon is also described by some as the power of accomplishment. Accomplishment causes your core attitude to become positive regarding the activity that was successful and because your core attitude feeds on itself it will tend to be more positive regarding other situations.

This is a very beneficial attribute of your core attitude when you are changing the behavior of your animal nature to enhance the positive expectations of your core attitude. Your core attitude will always duplicate the past. Unless you give your core attitude some reason to change, it will never change. It will continue to attract the kind of events it was taught to expect and when your attitude begins to attract positive events, it will continue to attract positive events.

Your core attitude's expectations are always self-fulfilling prophesies.

The relationship of your physical behavior to your attitude is more than close. Your physical behavior and your attitude always directly reflect each other.

Your animal brain always knows the kind of event that your attitude is expecting, for your brain is always expecting the past to repeat itself and it has recorded all of the events of your life. The behavior advised by your animal brain will always predict the event your attitude is expecting.

The behavior that your animal brain advises, be it bold, careful, confident, tentative, etc., will always be an absolutely accurate reflection of your attitude regarding any situation that you may be in, for it knows that your attitude always expects the past to repeat itself.

Your animal brain will not voluntarily change the behavior it is advising until your attitude starts to attract a different kind of event into your life, but you are in control of the behavior of the animal you inhabit.

Your animal brain cannot even suspect that it is the underlying positive or negative tone of the expectations of your attitude that has created and attracted all of the events in your life.

Only the mind of your Beingness can unravel the very, very secure prison that is your core attitude. It is the mind of your Beingness that can control the behavior of your animal nature.

You are imprisoned in whatever attitude you were taught to have and your attitude constantly produces the same kind of events for you to experience and your animal brain is constantly telling you, with its endless dialogue with you and the behavior it is advising, what to expect from future events which will always be the same kind of events you have always experienced. You are always on a treadmill of some degree of dissatisfaction and suffering.

How you physically respond to your animal brain's endless dialogue of advice and the physical behavior it advises, that are all intended by your animal nature to benefit you, is the secret to your escape from the prison that is your present attitude.

Your animal brain is constantly accurately informing you of what your attitude is expecting regarding every situation you are in and telling you what your response to those situations should be based on your attitude's present expectations and its advice will always predict the same kind of event that you have always experienced, but you can use that advice to change your attitude and the events of your life. If your behavior opposes the negativity of your core attitude, it will have a positive effect on your attitude; but your opposition must be choreographed so as not to cause your present attitude to experience fear intense enough to cause it to attract the event it fears. All of the power of your Beingness to create is trapped in the expectations of your present attitude. You have an animal attitude and fear is the mainstay of an animal attitude. It would be impossible for you to have an attitude that is without fear.

A healthy sense of fear is always a valuable attitude for almost every animal, but fear is the most detrimental of all human attitudes. Your animal brain is convinced that fear can cause you to prevent negative events from occurring or getting worse and so are you, but human fear, if it is intense enough, will attract the event that is feared. A positive response to dangerous situations is a very beneficial behavior for a human to take.

Once a human is taught to be fearful, its attitude will validate the value of fear by attracting fearful events and every human being is taught to be fearful.

Fear is the first attitude that you must diminish to create more positive events in your life.

You believe that fear is a valuable attitude because it causes you to take action to defend yourself from what you fear, but it is your fear that makes it necessary for you to defend yourself.

Changing your attitude to a more positive attitude is a monumental task. Your present attitude has validated all of its fears by attracting what it fears. Changing your attitude will invalidate all of the premises that you thought created the events of your life.

To change your attitude and the future events of your life requires that you abandon your personal history. Regurgitating the events of your life to other people only reinforces your attitude that created those events and you need to weaken the hold that your present attitude has over the events of your life. Your personal history is all about the validity of your present attitude. Your personal history that you dearly embrace, always promotes your present attitude that you need to change.

To change your attitude and the events of your life you must first conclude that there is a distinct possibility that your attitude could be creating and attracting the events you are experiencing. You must seriously consider the possibility that you may be a victim of your own making.

You are not a victim of those who taught you to have their attitude. They were trying to help you cope with the world. They believed that their attitude was the best possible attitude to have and why wouldn't they? Any human attitude will always validate itself. A human attitude is a very secure prison.

To change your attitude and thus the events of your life, it is necessary for you to take full responsibility for all of the events in your life. If you do not take full responsibility, there is no reason to change your attitude. Your present attitude has proven to be very accurate at predicting the flavor of the events in your life. It should be. It is attracting events with a flavor that matches its own positive or negative flavor. You are always a victim of your own attitude.

To improve your attitude, you must imagine how a more positive person would physically respond to whatever situation you are in. You must change your behavior to that of a more positive person.

When you respond physically, in any positive way to any situation you are in, you have improved your core attitude – you have caused it to morph to some degree and become more positive.

Your behavior has a direct effect on your attitude and the kind of event that it will attract, but the connection of a particular behavior (routine) to your present attitude can be difficult to recognize. Any change in your routines will affect your attitude in some way. You have developed behavioral patterns that match your attitude in every respect.

Changing your behavior must not cause you to experience intense fear, only a sense of discomfort. Discomfort is not an attitude that attracts negative events.

Changing your attitude will be a very gradual process. You must edge up to a more positive behavior without causing your present attitude to become excessively fearful of your new behavior.

It is easy to observe that the behavior of animals absolutely matches the ability of their physical attributes to handle whatever situation they are in. Your behavior needs to match the attitude you desire to have.

When you try to change your behavior to a more positive behavior, your animal brain will fight you every step of the way. It is totally comfortable with your present physical response to every situation no matter how negative it may be.

Causing your behavior to respond more positively to any situation with good results will cause your attitude to become more positive.

Understand this – your present attitude has been correct regarding all of the events of your life, which includes, on occasion, apparently preventing you from experiencing greater dissatisfaction and suffering. To change what has seemed to be a successful response to many situations in the past requires a pure understanding of the situation you are in, why you are in that situation, how you got into that situation and the impossibility of escaping that situation with your present attitude.

It will take some degree of courage to change your attitude, for your present attitude has proven it validity for your entire life. It has attracted all of the events in your life up to now. An attitude will normally only accept gradual change, but anything is possible for a fragment of Beingness.

THE ATTRIBUTES OF AN ENLIGHTENED ATTITUDE

Your attitude is who you believe you really are and causes you to become that person by attracting events that validate who you believe you are.

An enlightened attitude knows that it is attracting all of the events you are experiencing, without knowing or needing to know, in its absolute confidence, exactly what those events will be.

An enlightened attitude always requires you to do everything to the best of your ability. Any other response means you do not believe that you have control of the events you are experiencing, that you are a feather in the wind. Your attitude is the wind.

An enlightened attitude is honest and forthright knowing that it is attitude alone that creates events.

An enlightened attitude is not interested in its personal history, knowing that it was the product of an attitude that was infected with doubt and fear.

An enlightened attitude is always calm and confident knowing that there is nothing to fear.

An enlightened attitude is humble knowing that everyone is creating and attracting all of the events of their life.

An enlightened attitude does not experience self-importance, knowing that it is not competing with others for what it needs and desires. It knows that its only adversary is always its own negative expectations.

An enlightened attitude takes full responsibility for all of the events of its life.

An enlightened attitude avoids the fearful admonitions of the animal brain knowing that it is the guardian of the attitude that is the source of its dissatisfaction and suffering.

How would it feel like to have an enlightened attitude? Everyone has experienced the joy of a positive event. An absolutely positive attitude would expect every event to be positive.

An enlightened attitude would be like having a glowing ember of positive anticipation that is always about to ignite into a positive event and as the joy of each event expired, it would be replaced by the joy of anticipating the next positive event.

THE MUCH-MALIGNED EGO

Everybody attacks the ego. Yet it is the most dominant attitude in the world in which you struggle. In simple, direct terms, the ego is just a take care of yourself first attitude in whatever situation that you find yourself. It is an important and valuable animal attribute. An animal instinctually knows that it must take care of itself. This is the most beneficial attitude that an animal can have.

The survival of an animal in the limited, competitive and dangerous world of Nature is very dependent on an animal providing for and protecting itself. It is dangerous for an animal to have any other attitude. The ego is the law of the jungle applied to the society in which humans struggle.

Animals cannot be criticized for being self-centered. It is their most valuable attribute for survival, but when this attitude is given control of the intelligence and creativity of Beingness, it can be very destructive to others and was intended to have this effect.

The only exception to this self-centered animal attitude is in regards to an animal's offspring. Animals will risk injury and even death to protect their offspring, but this is not a contradiction of their self-centered attitude, for an animal instinctually views its offspring as an extension of itself. It is really taking care of itself when it takes care of its offspring. This is especially true of females, for it is from their body that their offspring emerge.

You have two natures and one of those natures is an animal, and the attitude of that animal will always be self-centered. That attitude can only be controlled. It cannot be radically changed or eliminated for it is that animal's instinct to have such an attitude. Your animal nature's me first attitude is as natural as your body's need to sweat when it is too hot.

Humans are imprisoned in their animal nature's self-centered world by their attitude.

RECONCILING THE CONFLICT OF THE ABSOLUTE FREEDOM AND THE ABSOLUTE ONENESS OF BEINGNESS

To fully understand your Beingness, it is necessary to reconcile the absolute freedom of Beingness with the absolute oneness of Beingness, for freedom produces diversity, but oneness has no diversity. How does Beingness simultaneously experience these contradictory attributes?

Beingness must have two different states of Being. The primordial dormant state of Beingness is its state of absolute oneness and absolute potential to imagine and create and its other state of Being is when it is imagining, creating and experiencing what it has imagined. Your Beingness is in the imagining, creating and experiencing state of Beingness.

From the fact that whatever the energy in the world of Nature becomes, it always returns to its original state of pure indistinguishable energy with the potential to become anything, it can be concluded that Beingness prefers the absolute oneness of its state of pure potential to imagine and create, to its state of imagining and creating, that Beingness prefers the absolute harmony of the absolute oneness of its state of limitless potential to imagine and create, to its state of imagining and creating.

If this is true, what causes Beingness to imagine and create?

If the oneness of its limitless potential at rest is its preferred state of Being, as the constant reversion of everything that exists in the world of Nature back to being indistinguishable energy strongly suggests, Beingness could not desire to fragment and thereby abandon its primordial state of absolute oneness and absolute satisfaction.

It must then be the nature of Primordial Beingness to fragment. It does not decide to fragment. It is simply the nature of Primordial Beingness to sometimes fragment and it must then be the nature of a fragment of Beingness to imagine, create and experience what it imagines.

What then is the source of the fragments of Beingness that become humans?

In the absolute freedom and potential of a fragment of Beingness, it could simply desire to fragment so that, in its oneness with any fragment of its Beingness, it could experience as real through that fragment the reality it had imagined and experience the joy of first experiencing and then overcoming or escaping from that reality to the absolute freedom and oneness of its nature.

The universal continuous reversion of the matter and life in the world of Nature back to being the pure energy, from which it came to be, seems to symbolize the inevitable return of every fragment of Beingness back to its primordial dormant state of absolute oneness and potential. Why would a fragment of Beingness desire to return to this state of Being?

The static, changeless state of absolute oneness and dormant potential could not create joy, but it produces endless absolute satisfaction.

It would seem that the joy of imagining, creating, experiencing and then escaping from what it has imagined can never satisfy Beingness.

Joy to Beingness seems to be much like chocolate is to humans and satisfaction is to Beingness much like sustenance is to humans.

The final action of any fragment of Beingness would always be to return to its primordial state of absolute potential, oneness and satisfaction.

When a fragment of Beingness abandons its imagining and creating to again experience the absolute oneness and absolute satisfaction of its primordial existence, it would seem that all of the primordial existence of Beingness in its absolute oneness would experience with that fragment the joy it would experience from that return to absolute satisfaction. This would be the ultimate joy that Beingness could ever experience and would never end.

WISDOM

The older you are the more knowledge your brain will have regarding the kind of events you can expect from your attitude and the wiser you will be about the events that your attitude creates.

One person's wisdom regarding the effect of their attitude is only of value to another person if they have the same attitude and many people do have the same attitude.

Children, the more they mature, the more they discover from the events that their attitudes create and attract, how wise their parents are, for it is almost always from their parents that most people are taught to have their attitude and their parents have lived with their attitude for a long time and are far more aware of the kind of events that their attitude creates and attracts. It takes a while for their children to come to this full realization.

Everyone eventually becomes wise regarding what events their particular attitude creates and attracts for they are constantly experiencing the effect of their attitude on the events of their life.

True Wisdom is to know how you are creating, attracting and affecting every event in your life.

HOW BEINGNESS EXPRESSES LOVE

In its absolute oneness, Beingness is always dealing with itself and will, in love of self, always give itself total freedom and will in love of self always harmonize with that freedom.

The world of Nature provides the most vivid picture of that love. Every species of life in Nature, in an expression of that love, has been given the ability to express its nature without preventing any other species of life from expressing its nature. Each species of life has been given attributes that prevent other species of life from stopping it from expressing its nature.

It is only necessary for a single member of a species of life to survive and express its nature for the entire species to have successfully expressed its freedom to express its nature, for each species is in essence a singular form of life.

Predators do not prevent their prey from expressing their nature, for their prey is harmoniously given attributes that either enable it to sometimes avoid predators or the ability to procreate more of its species than predators can consume.

Both the predator and its prey are given the freedom to express their natures. Each species is given the attributes that allow them to successfully express their nature without preventing other species of life from expressing their natures.

Your attitude is your nature as a human being and you always successfully express your attitude, for the reality in which you have imprisoned yourself always validates whatever attitude you have. This is an expression of the love of Beingness.

You willingly agreed to being raised to have a particular species of attitude and that attitude caused the reality in which you are imprisoned to harmoniously validate that attitude. Your Beingness chooses your brand of attitude before you were born by choosing the humans that would be your parents.

You are expressing the nature of Beingness when it is imprisoned in an animal body in a limited, negative reality and forced to have a particular attitude that creates and attracts events that validate that attitude.

THE ULTIMATE CONCLUSION –
BEING IS ITS OWN MEANING

The events that each fragment of Beingness attracts, creates and experiences is personal to that fragment of Beingness and has no effect on the events that other fragments of Beingness may be attracting, creating and experiencing, even though those events may seem to affect other fragments of Beingness, for an event created by one fragment of Beingness can be a perfect match to an event that the attitude of another fragment of Beingness imprisoned in the same reality is expecting and thereby demanding and attracting.

You create or attract to you the events that your attitude is demanding. Because of this, whatever a fragment of Beingness experiences has meaning only to that fragment of Beingness. Fragments of Beingness create meaning by experiencing the events that they imagine, attract and create but only for themselves. Being is its own meaning and this is the only meaning there is or there will ever be.

Fragments of Beingness can be subject to the events created by other fragments of Beingness, but only if their attitude causes themselves to be subject to those events.

Each fragment of Beingness creates meaning, but only for itself.

You and you alone gave the meaning to every event in your life, for you created, attracted and affected all of the events of your life with your attitude.

If everyone is creating, attracting and affecting all of the events they are experiencing with their attitude, then whatever meaning there is or will ever be, to the events of their individual lives, it will have no meaning to other fragments of Beingness unless in their absolute freedom they cause it to have meaning by causing themselves to also experience those events.

Since everyone is attracting and creating the events they experience, everyone is always creating the meaning of their life by experiencing what they attract and create. An event does not have meaning unless it is experienced by a fragment of Beingness.

Meaning is not about good and evil. It is about the creation of experiences and the dissatisfaction, suffering, satisfaction and joy that those experiences cause a fragment of Beingness to experience when it is not experiencing the ultimate satisfaction of the absolute harmonic oneness and potential of its primordial nature.

No matter what event that a fragment of Beingness imagines, creates or attracts, it always creates joy, either from what it experiences or by escaping from what it caused itself to experience.

Since every event created by Beingness eventually creates joy, it can be concluded that the creation of joy is the only purpose of what Beingness imagines and creates.